THE BEST UNICORN COLOURING BOOK

for Little Boys and Girls

BY

PODIUM

HTTPS://LEARN.PODIUM.SCHOOL

Karkadann In The Night

Unicorn And Rainbow

Butterfly Winged Unicorn

Beautiful Winged Unicorn

Among Us Unicorn

Shopkin Unicorn

Bella In The Night

Bella From Unicorn

Bella Unicorn

Unicorn Sitting

Unicorn's Face

Unicorn In The Forest

Strong Unicorn

Simple Unicorn

Magical Baby Unicorn

Beautiful Unicorn Shining

Sweet Unicorn

Unicorn With Clubs Symbol

Unicorn Seeing

Unicorn Running Fast

Unicorn With Heart On Horn

Cute Fat Unicorn On Leaf

Unicorn With Stars

Simple Unicorn's Head

Evil Unicorn

Cute Baby Unicorn

Unicorn Sleeping In The Cloud

Happy Unicorn

Cute Unicorn

Lovely Unicorn

The Mighty Unicorn

Rarity Unicorn

Twins Unicorn

Unicorn In The Wood

Little Cute Unicorn

Unicorn With Fairy

Beautiful Lady And Unicorn

Baby Cute Gillter Eyes Unicorn

Cute Unicorn With Heart

Unicorn With Beautiful Glitter Eyes

Unicorn With Wreath

Girl Sleeping With Unicorn

Beautiful Unicorn Shining

Lovely Unicorn Looking

Little Unicorn

Hyperactive Unicorn

Unicorn Cupcake

Unicorn Running

Girl With Unicorn

Little Unicorn On Cloud

Unicorn Playing Guitar

Little Unicorn On Cupcake

Baby Unicorn With A Balloon

Beautiful Unicorn Head

Winged Unicorn

Little Unicorn With Balloons

Awesome Unicorn

Unicorn Vs Narwhal

Unicorn Sitting On Cloud

Unicorn With Bow At Tail

Fairy And Unicorn

Winged Unicorn And Flowers

Unicorn Wearing Crown

Little Unicorn Sleeping

Unicorn Head And Flowers

Chibi Unicorn

Cute Little Unicorn

Unicorn Jumping

Awesome Unicorn Head

Unicorn With Star

Unicorn And Witch

Unicorn Head With Rainbow

Baby Unicorn In Magical Sky

Unicorn In Cage

Couple Unicorn

Unicorn Moving

A Couple On Unicorn

Little Unicorn And Rainbow

Girl Giving Apple For Unicorn

Unicorn Sat Down

A Thin Unicorn

Unicorn Having Fun

Unicorn Standing On Cloud

A Couple Unicorn

Birthday Of Unicorn

Baby Unicorn Sleeping

Happy Face Unicorn

Unicorn Head And Roses

Baby Unicorn Flying

Unicorn With A Shooting Star

Unicorn And The Castle

Sticker Unicorn

Unicorn Head Smiling

Unicorn And Stars Around

Unicorn Eating Hierba

Spotted Unicorn Running

Unicorn Has Cute Wings